THE
CHALLENGE
JOURNAL

30 DAYS OF
DISCIPLINE. HABITS. CHANGE.

JAKE GREENBERG & JUSTIN SUTHERLIN

THE CHALLENGE JOURNAL by Jake Greenberg & Justin Sutherlin

Published by CHALLENGE PROJECT, LLC

www.ChallengeProject.com

Copyright © 2021 CHALLENGE PROJECT, LLC

All rights reserved. Except as permitted under the United States Copyright Act of 1976, no part of this publication may be reproduced, distributed, or transmitted in any form or by any means, including photocopying, recording, or other electronic or mechanical methods, or stored in a database or retrieval system without the prior written permission of the author or publisher, except in the case of brief quotations embodied in critical reviews and certain other noncommercial uses permitted by copyright law.

ISBN: 978-0-578-33179-9

Printed in the United States of America

Second Edition

For permissions or more information, please visit
www.ChallengeProject.com

TABLE OF CONTENTS

INTRODUCTION	3
HOW TO USE THIS JOURNAL	5
WHAT	7
WHY	9
HOW	10
WHEN	11
TIPS FOR GREAT SUCCESS	12
CHALLENGES VS. GOALS	14
CHALLENGE CONTRACT	15
PROGRESS TRACKER	17
DEFINE YOUR CHALLENGES	18
DAY TRACKER	21
10 DAY ASSESSMENT	31
20 DAY ASSESSMENT	42
30 DAY ASSESSMENT	53
OMEGA & ALPHA	55
NOTES	57

> "THE ONLY PERSON YOU ARE DESTINED TO BECOME IS THE PERSON YOU DECIDE TO BE."
>
> — RALPH WALDO EMERSON

INTRODUCTION

Do you need to read all this? No. Will it help immensely? You decide.

The person you are today is the product of every decision you have ever made and experience you have ever had. Don't make excuses; just own it. Once you accept it, you can change it. The fact that you're holding this journal in your hands says you want something better for yourself.

In today's culture, people are often so quick to reference external circumstances, past experiences, and fears of the future to justify their current position and trajectory. Do you know what's behind all those objections? Excuses and a lack of accountability. Most people don't want to take ownership of their shortcomings and failures, nor do they want to experience the discomfort of creating the discipline to change them. The past does affect us, but it does not define us. Past trauma and future adverse circumstances should inspire you to prepare yourself now so you can mitigate them when they ultimately do come. Take responsibility and become disciplined.

Life is a game of inches. It is a process of laying bricks and casting votes every day and through every decision. Contrary to popular belief, we are not established or brought down by major defining moments. Instead, we are either created or destroyed by the little choices we make daily. In all reality, these make up the majority of our life's trajectory, journey, and destination.

Although you can cheat in life, there is no cheating life itself. Make no mistake about it, although these definitions have somewhat subjective meanings to each individual, you're either winning or losing. You know which side you're on. You either pay now or pay later. It's inevitable. As famous speaker and entrepreneur Jim Rohn once said, *"There are two pains in life: the pain of discipline and the pain of regret.*

INTRODUCTION

Discipline weighs ounces; regret weighs tons." That's the entire purpose of this journal: to pay the price of discipline now instead of regret later.

In the words of the successful business owner and motivational speaker Les Brown, *"If you do what is easy, your life will be hard. But if you do what is hard, your life will be easy."* His wise words couldn't be more accurate.

Most of us have heard the question, "How do you eat an elephant?" The correct answer is, "One bite at a time." This principle is true in every area of our lives. "THE CHALLENGE JOURNAL" is meant to help you dissect your elephant down into bite-sized pieces. The lessons from this adage will be a theme carried throughout this journal.

"THE CHALLENGE JOURNAL" is intended to inspire discipline, provide accountability, and measure growth through incremental and sustainable actions in your daily life. This will eventually produce massive, life-changing growth and a person worth becoming. The future will become the vista you use to look back on how far you've come, as well as where you're going.

We all want to improve our lives in one way or another. However, people don't want to know what is true; they want to know what is possible. If you're holding this journal in your hands, you already know what is true, and you're far more interested in what is possible. The fact is, you're not where you want to be...yet.

HOW TO USE THIS JOURNAL

This journal was designed to be simple, straight forward, and easy to use. Here's what you need to know...

At the beginning of every 30 days, you're going to be setting some challenges for yourself. These should be actions we take on a daily basis that "move the needle forward" and lead us to our goals, dreams, and ambitions. This journal limits you to setting four challenges, which is intentional. You may want to set even fewer than four challenges, but do not set more. Setting more than four challenges will divide your attention, energy, and effort and make you far less likely to succeed.

Be hyper-focused and hyper-specific. Set "S.M.A.R.T." challenges. This approach takes all the ambiguity out of the process. "S.M.A.R.T." stands for:

S: SPECIFIC
M: MEASURABLE
A: ACHIEVABLE
R: REALISTIC
T: TIMELY

This journal is set up in a very simple, yet unique format. We call it the "What- Why- How- When" Challenge Frame. Just like a house or box gets its strength and structure from its shape, the same is true of the Challenge Frame. Here is a visual:

> **REASONS BEFORE RESULTS; PROCESS BEFORE THE PRIZE.**

"WHAT"

"What" refers to the specific challenges you have chosen to complete. They are the daily actions that move you forward and add up overtime. "What" is where we establish S.M.A.R.T. challenges, eliminating ambiguity. When programmed correctly, it gives a very clear standard to determine if a challenge is fully completed or failed.

"What" requires you to think about how you want to challenge yourself, where you want to go, what you want to achieve, and most importantly, who you want to become. This should be accomplished with a "reverse engineering" approach by determining where your desired "Step Z" is – the future – and working your way back to "Step A" – the present.

We also believe in consequences, both positive and negative. Positive consequences of accomplishing your challenges might be mental fortitude, grit, financial freedom, improved health and fitness, more confidence, better relationships, personal growth and knowledge, deeper faith, or any of the other rewards you get from the process or end result. However, we live in a world where consequences can also be negative, often referred to as "penalties".

Every cause has an effect; every action has a result. There are the results of either commission or omission. Commission is doing something you were not supposed to do. Omission is not doing something you were supposed to do. Either way, if the right thing is not done, there needs to be a penalty.

In the same way that rewards incentivize good behavior, penalties can also deter bad behavior. Otherwise, what's the harm in not doing the right thing? Fear of a penalty can and should be harnessed to stay on track.

"WHAT"

With that said, we are challenging you to set your own penalties for not staying true to your commitments. The results of inaction over the course of years or your lifetime compound greatly. However, the delayed effect rarely compels immediate and sustained change. This is why you need to program immediate and sustained penalties into your challenges. Discipline, consistency, and proper prioritizing get rewarded while laziness, inconsistency, and poor prioritizing get penalized. "What" not only encompasses the specifics of the challenges you choose, but also specifies exactly what will happen if you break your commitment for any reason.

If you do fail, pay your penalty and get back on track. Treat your penalties as the cost to buy back in.

If you don't consistently complete your challenges, the penalty aspect is more than just saying, "Oh well", and moving on with the same ineffective habits, patterns, rituals, and disciplines that got you to where you are now. Your penalties should suck. Enough said.

"What" defines the elephant you want to eat, what bite size pieces look like, and the penalties for not eating the elephant.

"WHY"

"Why" is the compelling reason for choosing to complete your challenges. First, deeply contemplate the emotions that you have for your current situation in life. Now, harness the feelings you will have once you achieve your challenges. Intentionally remember all of those feelings for the future. They will be a major catalyst for change and sustainability, as well as serving as an undeniable progress report for the future.

Challenges need to be backed by conviction in order to fuel discipline and sustainability. This is where the "Why" comes in. The purpose of a challenge is not to achieve a temporary accomplishment, but rather to fundamentally change your current self into the future self you want to become.

"Why" is important for establishing the initial motivation for wanting to achieve your challenges. More importantly, it supersedes motivation, which is extrinsic, and immediately focuses on the discipline and core beliefs, which are your intrinsic convictions behind your challenges. If your "Why" is deeply compelling, it should inspire accountability and act as race fuel when obstacles, decisions, inconveniences, or laziness inevitably show up.

"Why" should be the most abstract, subjective, and emotive section compared to the "What", "How", and "When" portions of the Challenge Frame.

"Why" is your intrinsic motivation to start, continue, and finish eating your elephant – even when you're full or tired of eating.

"HOW"

"How" refers to the habits, patterns, rituals, and disciplines you will use to accomplish your challenges.

A challenge is what you want to achieve. A system is how you plan to achieve it. Goals are the destination; systems are the journey. "How" is the implementation of clear, actionable steps to complete your "What". It takes theory and turns it into practicality: "How" = Action.

"How" takes into consideration the negatives – obstacles, inconveniences, and excuses – and implements strategies to eliminate them. It also pre-plans how you can re-position yourself for success through convenience.

"How" is where a specific strategy or gameplan is made, comprised of clear actionable steps. This forces you to think about and plan your actions with specific behaviors and imposed limitations. Here you switch from being a reactive person to a proactive person.

"How" is the opposite of the reverse engineering process mentioned in the "What" section. Rather than starting at your desired future destination – Step Z – and strategizing your way backward to the present – Step A –, the "How" establishes where you are now – Step A –, where you want to go – Step Z –, and how you plan to move forward – Steps B through Y. Remember this is called a "challenge" journal for a reason: it's meant to challenge you. With that said, you must balance challenge with sustainability. Use this diagram to provide a good visual:

↓EXCESSIVELY EASY↓	↓SWEET SPOT↓	↓EXCESSIVELY DIFFICULT↓
UNCHALLENGING --------	CHALLENGING BUT SUSTAINABLE	-------- UNSUSTAINABLE

"How" is the specific way you plan to eat your elephant, bite by bite, from start to finish.

"WHEN"

"When" is the time frame your challenges must be completed within. It gives the challenges a definitive end date. The challenges most people set lack a time frame or deadline. Many of the challenges or goals that do have end dates are usually so far away that it's usually forgotten or unadhered to (think new years resolutions, 5 year goals, 10 year plans, etc).

They are too macro when we need to be focusing on micro. Long term aspirations are great and highly encouraged, but they must be broken down into smaller time frames and objectives.

This journal is structured using multiple time frames. First, the parameter for this CHALLENGE JOURNAL is 30 days. It is broken down into 30 one day challenge logs with an assessment every 10 days.

At the end of the 30 DAY CHALLENGE you get the opportunity to plan and continue your progress and momentum into the next 30 DAY CHALLENGE. As you can see, forward planning and reflective assessments are key components of this journal.

"When" provides the time frame for eating your "elephant" and the date by which it needs to be completely consumed.

TIPS FOR GREAT SUCCESS

1. ACCOUNTABILITY PARTNER(S) - We highly recommend that you do this challenge with at least one accountability partner. Make sure whoever you choose is someone you genuinely would not want to let down, embarrass, or disappoint.

2. MARK THE "X" - Actually cross off each accomplished day of the 30 day checkboxes on page 17 of this journal. The reward of seeing an unbroken string of "X's" will provide immediate gratification, accountability to maintain the success streak, and a quick snapshot of measurable success for both these 30 days and in the future looking back.

3. CHALLENGE CATEGORIES - Fitness/Health, Personal, Professional, & Spiritual. If you want to get better in any of these areas, you should be challenging yourself in them. These are just suggestions, but they will help make you more comprehensive.

4. SET PENALTIES - Before you start, set penalties for not completing your set challenges consistently. They should suck. If you fail, pay the price and get back on track. This is your cost to "buy back in." This will keep you afraid of failing or not completing it, as well as help you set achievable challenges for yourself. Never allow yourself to make the same mistake or fail twice in a row. For example, if your challenge is to run two miles each day and you didn't do it, then your penalty to "buy back in" could be that you have to run six miles the next day (it's supposed to suck).

5. HABIT STACKING - Combine existing habits with new ones. Either add the new habits to the beginning or end of your current habits. The existing habits become prompts for the new ones. For example, if you're challenging yourself to pray or meditate more often, then designate the first minute of every meal or every drive you make to nothing but praying or meditating.

TIPS FOR GREAT SUCCESS

6. IF/THEN - Set your challenges and penalties using "if/then". If I do/don't _____, then I will/won't _____. This is all about cause and effect. This could be used for both good or bad consequences.

7. MAKE THE RIGHT STUFF EASY - Make the desirable behaviors and habits obvious and convenient. Remove any obstacles in your way beforehand so completing your challenges is easy to do.

8. MAKE THE WRONG STUFF HARD - Make the bad habits, temptations, and distractions inconvenient and out of sight, out of mind. Make them hard, labor intensive, or embarrassing.

9. USE TIME AND LOCATION PROMPTS - These can help you set benchmarks and reminders for your challenges. Eventually you will begin to think of times and locations synonymously with your challenges.

10. OTHER CRITICAL DAILY TASKS (CDT's) - Either the night before or first thing in the morning each day you'll have the option to list other Critical Daily Tasks (CDT's) that you need to complete that day in addition to your daily challenges. These are standalone tasks that will have a direct impact on either eliminating serious problems or making serious moves forward. Decide these by thinking to yourself, "Today would be a great day if I could accomplish these things..." Completing each task produces momentum for not only that day, but your entire journey of living a successful and fulfilling life. This is not merely a shopping or to-do list.

11. KEEP THE MOMENTUM - Don't stop after one 30 DAY CHALLENGE. One isolated 30 day period of hard work and success will be meaningless in the grand scheme of things if you don't maintain and continue it. Think of continuing your discipline as casting votes or laying the foundation for the person you want to be, one vote or brick at a time.

CHALLENGES VS. GOALS

In this journal you are to focus on creating CHALLENGES for yourself that are designed to achieve your GOALS. Below is a chart we've created to help you distinguish between what would be considered a CHALLENGE vs. a GOAL. Challenges don't replace goals; they support them.

	CHALLENGES	GOALS
WHAT	Identity and process based.	Outcome based.
GOAL	Better than you were yesterday. Focuses on the person you want to become.	Lofty perfection standard; anything subpar is failure.
TIME	Present based; usually on a daily, weekly, or monthly basis.	Future based; often distant.
COMPLEXITY	Simple, singular action.	Could be very complex and require multiple actions.
SUSTAINABILITY	Usually much more manageable. Produces momentum and discipline with daily completion.	Frequently overwhelming. Difficult to maintain momentum and discipline long term.
PRACTICALITY	Bite sized pieces that add up over time, leading you to your goals and desired identity.	Specifies where you want to go and what you want to achieve.
SUCCESS	Enjoys the process and sets the bar at the "majority wins" (Ex: voting or sports scoreboard). Self improvement.	Soley based on achievement.
FAILURE	Immediate awareness of success or failure based on completion within the designated time frame. This provides opportunity to immediately recover if daily, weekly, or monthly failure does occur.	Sets up substantial room for failure, even if one rep, dollar, mile, minute, page, ounce, etc. short. "All or nothing" standard. Can be less specific unless set as S.M.A.R.T. goals.
GRATIFICATION	Usually immediate and sustained because the challenges are completed daily, weekly, or monthly. It produces momentum.	Usually delayed and long term, meaning you will not be happy until you get there or achieve that. Difficult to sustain momentum.

CHALLENGE CONTRACT

I, _____ (*Your Name*), am making a personal contract with myself to begin this 30 DAY CHALLENGE on _____ (*Start Date*).

I am dedicating myself to not only participate in, but to completing this challenge in its entirety. I will choose up to 4 challenges. Each challenge is something I am deeply moved by and committed to. I will also choose a penalty for not completing each challenge in its entirety, every day for the next 30 consecutive days. These penalties are not optional. I choose to accept their discomfort and pain in full.

I have thought about the person I want to become, the character I desire to develop, and the challenge(s) I am committed to accomplishing. I am committed to changing the person I am today into who I want to be tomorrow. This will set the stage for the rest of my life. I do not take this commitment, these challenge(s), or penalties lightly.

My word, integrity, and destiny are on the line. Failure and inconsistency compromise all of them. I choose to change. I choose to be disciplined. I choose to be committed. Inconvenience, lack of motivation, peer pressure, long days, tired nights, and laziness will not be permitted as valid excuses. Weakness is a choice, and I choose to reject it.

The past does not define me; the future does. I accept the responsibility that tomorrow is created and shaped by today. I choose the uphill, narrow, rocky, and lonely road to greatness. I will push hard when things are easy, and even harder when they are not. "I should" just became "I shall." "I want" is now "I will."

CHALLENGE CONTRACT

☐ I choose to complete this 30 DAY CHALLENGE with the comradery of my accountability partner, _____ *(Accountability Partner's Name)*. I have informed them of the details of my challenge, including my "What's," "Why's," "How's," and "When's." They understand the gravity and seriousness of my commitment to these challenges and are committed to my success and growth over my comfort and feelings.

☐ I choose to go at this 30 DAY CHALLENGE alone, knowing every success or failure is solely on me. My "What's," "Why's," "How's," and "When's" are specific and strong enough to pull me forward and push me through despite any adversities that can and will arise.

X _____ Date: _____
       Your Signature

X _____ Date: _____
  Accountability Partner's Signature

PROGRESS TRACKER

MARK AN "X" ON EACH COMPLETED DAY

1	2	3	4	5
6	7	8	9	10
11	12	13	14	15
16	17	18	19	20
21	22	23	24	25
26	27	28	29	30

DEFINE YOUR CHALLENGES

CHALLENGE #1

☐ FITNESS/HEALTH ☐ PERSONAL ☐ PROFESSIONAL ☐ SPIRITUAL ☐ OTHER _____

WHAT _____
_____
_____

WHY _____
_____
_____

HOW _____
_____
_____

PENALTY _____
_____
_____

CHALLENGE #2

☐ FITNESS/HEALTH ☐ PERSONAL ☐ PROFESSIONAL ☐ SPIRITUAL ☐ OTHER _____

WHAT _____
_____
_____

WHY _____
_____
_____

HOW _____
_____
_____

PENALTY _____
_____
_____

DEFINE YOUR CHALLENGES

CHALLENGE #3

☐ FITNESS/HEALTH ☐ PERSONAL ☐ PROFESSIONAL ☐ SPIRITUAL ☐ OTHER _____

WHAT _____
_____
_____

WHY _____
_____
_____

HOW _____
_____
_____

PENALTY _____
_____
_____

CHALLENGE #4

☐ FITNESS/HEALTH ☐ PERSONAL ☐ PROFESSIONAL ☐ SPIRITUAL ☐ OTHER _____

WHAT _____
_____
_____

WHY _____
_____
_____

HOW _____
_____
_____

PENALTY _____
_____
_____

> "IF YOU WANT SOMETHING YOU'VE NEVER HAD, YOU MUST BE WILLING TO DO SOMETHING YOU'VE NEVER DONE."

___/___/ 20___

DAY TRACKER

DAY 1 OF 30

MARK AN "X" ON EACH COMPLETED CHALLENGE

CHALLENGE: #1 ☐ #2 ☐ #3 ☐ #4 ☐

DIFFICULTY LEVEL (1-10)

CHALLENGE: #1 _____ #2 _____ #3 _____ #4 _____

TIME TO COMPLETE (IF APPLICABLE)

CHALLENGE: #1 _____ #2 _____ #3 _____ #4 _____

REFLECT ON TODAY'S CHALLENGES

REFLECTIONS _____

_____
_____
_____
_____
_____
_____
_____
_____
_____
_____
_____
_____
_____

TODAY'S OTHER CRITICAL DAILY TASKS (CDT'S)

☐ _____
☐ _____
☐ _____
☐ _____

___/___/ 20___ **DAY TRACKER** DAY 2 OF 30

MARK AN "X" ON EACH COMPLETED CHALLENGE

CHALLENGE: #1 ☐ #2 ☐ #3 ☐ #4 ☐

DIFFICULTY LEVEL (1-10)

CHALLENGE: #1 _____ #2 _____ #3 _____ #4 _____

TIME TO COMPLETE (IF APPLICABLE)

CHALLENGE: #1 _____ #2 _____ #3 _____ #4 _____

REFLECT ON TODAY'S CHALLENGES

REFLECTIONS _____

_____

_____

_____

_____

_____

_____

_____

_____

_____

_____

_____

_____

TODAY'S OTHER CRITICAL DAILY TASKS (CDT'S)

☐ _____
☐ _____
☐ _____
☐ _____

___/___/ 20___

DAY TRACKER

DAY 3 OF 30

MARK AN "X" ON EACH COMPLETED CHALLENGE

CHALLENGE: #1 ☐   #2 ☐   #3 ☐   #4 ☐

DIFFICULTY LEVEL (1-10)

CHALLENGE: #1 _____   #2 _____   #3 _____   #4 _____

TIME TO COMPLETE (IF APPLICABLE)

CHALLENGE: #1 _____   #2 _____   #3 _____   #4 _____

REFLECT ON TODAY'S CHALLENGES

REFLECTIONS _____

_____
_____
_____
_____
_____
_____
_____
_____
_____
_____
_____
_____

TODAY'S OTHER CRITICAL DAILY TASKS (CDT'S)

☐ _____
☐ _____
☐ _____
☐ _____

___/___/ 20___   **DAY TRACKER**   DAY 4 OF 30

MARK AN "X" ON EACH COMPLETED CHALLENGE

CHALLENGE: #1 ☐   #2 ☐   #3 ☐   #4 ☐

DIFFICULTY LEVEL (1-10)

CHALLENGE: #1 _____   #2 _____   #3 _____   #4 _____

TIME TO COMPLETE (IF APPLICABLE)

CHALLENGE: #1 _____   #2 _____   #3 _____   #4 _____

REFLECT ON TODAY'S CHALLENGES

REFLECTIONS _____

_____

_____

_____

_____

_____

_____

_____

_____

_____

_____

_____

_____

TODAY'S OTHER CRITICAL DAILY TASKS (CDT'S)

☐ _____
☐ _____
☐ _____
☐ _____

___/___/ 20___ **DAY TRACKER** DAY 5 OF 30

MARK AN "X" ON EACH COMPLETED CHALLENGE

CHALLENGE: #1 ☐   #2 ☐   #3 ☐   #4 ☐

DIFFICULTY LEVEL (1-10)

CHALLENGE: #1 _____   #2 _____   #3 _____   #4 _____

TIME TO COMPLETE (IF APPLICABLE)

CHALLENGE: #1 _____   #2 _____   #3 _____   #4 _____

REFLECT ON TODAY'S CHALLENGES

REFLECTIONS _____

_____
_____
_____
_____
_____
_____
_____
_____
_____
_____
_____
_____

TODAY'S OTHER CRITICAL DAILY TASKS (CDT'S)

☐ _____
☐ _____
☐ _____
☐ _____

___/___/ 20___

DAY TRACKER

DAY 6 OF 30

MARK AN "X" ON EACH COMPLETED CHALLENGE

CHALLENGE: #1 ☐   #2 ☐   #3 ☐   #4 ☐

DIFFICULTY LEVEL (1-10)

CHALLENGE: #1 _____   #2 _____   #3 _____   #4 _____

TIME TO COMPLETE (IF APPLICABLE)

CHALLENGE: #1 _____   #2 _____   #3 _____   #4 _____

REFLECT ON TODAY'S CHALLENGES

REFLECTIONS _____

_____
_____
_____
_____
_____
_____
_____
_____
_____
_____
_____
_____

TODAY'S OTHER CRITICAL DAILY TASKS (CDT'S)

☐ _____
☐ _____
☐ _____
☐ _____

___/___/ 20___ **DAY TRACKER** DAY 7 OF 30

MARK AN "X" ON EACH COMPLETED CHALLENGE

CHALLENGE: #1 ☐ #2 ☐ #3 ☐ #4 ☐

DIFFICULTY LEVEL (1-10)

CHALLENGE: #1 _____ #2 _____ #3 _____ #4 _____

TIME TO COMPLETE (IF APPLICABLE)

CHALLENGE: #1 _____ #2 _____ #3 _____ #4 _____

REFLECT ON TODAY'S CHALLENGES

REFLECTIONS _____

_____

_____

_____

_____

_____

_____

_____

_____

_____

_____

_____

_____

TODAY'S OTHER CRITICAL DAILY TASKS (CDT'S)

☐ _____
☐ _____
☐ _____
☐ _____

___/___/ 20___   **DAY TRACKER**   DAY 8 OF 30

MARK AN "X" ON EACH COMPLETED CHALLENGE

CHALLENGE: #1 ☐   #2 ☐   #3 ☐   #4 ☐

DIFFICULTY LEVEL (1-10)

CHALLENGE: #1 _____   #2 _____   #3 _____   #4 _____

TIME TO COMPLETE (IF APPLICABLE)

CHALLENGE: #1 _____   #2 _____   #3 _____   #4 _____

REFLECT ON TODAY'S CHALLENGES

REFLECTIONS _____

_____

_____

_____

_____

_____

_____

_____

_____

_____

_____

_____

_____

TODAY'S OTHER CRITICAL DAILY TASKS (CDT'S)

☐ _____
☐ _____
☐ _____
☐ _____

___/___/ 20___

DAY TRACKER

DAY 9 OF 30

MARK AN "X" ON EACH COMPLETED CHALLENGE

CHALLENGE: #1 ☐   #2 ☐   #3 ☐   #4 ☐

DIFFICULTY LEVEL (1-10)

CHALLENGE: #1 _____   #2 _____   #3 _____   #4 _____

TIME TO COMPLETE (IF APPLICABLE)

CHALLENGE: #1 _____   #2 _____   #3 _____   #4 _____

REFLECT ON TODAY'S CHALLENGES

REFLECTIONS _____

_____
_____
_____
_____
_____
_____
_____
_____
_____
_____
_____
_____

TODAY'S OTHER CRITICAL DAILY TASKS (CDT'S)

☐ _____
☐ _____
☐ _____
☐ _____

___/___/ 20___ **DAY TRACKER** DAY 10 OF 30

MARK AN "X" ON EACH COMPLETED CHALLENGE

CHALLENGE: #1 ☐   #2 ☐   #3 ☐   #4 ☐

DIFFICULTY LEVEL (1-10)

CHALLENGE: #1 _____   #2 _____   #3 _____   #4 _____

TIME TO COMPLETE (IF APPLICABLE)

CHALLENGE: #1 _____   #2 _____   #3 _____   #4 _____

REFLECT ON TODAY'S CHALLENGES

REFLECTIONS _____

_____

_____

_____

_____

_____

_____

_____

_____

_____

_____

_____

_____

TODAY'S OTHER CRITICAL DAILY TASKS (CDT'S)

☐ _____
☐ _____
☐ _____
☐ _____

10 DAY ASSESSMENT

DAY 10 OF 30

You're 1/3 of the way to completing this 30 DAY CHALLENGE. Now is a great time to reflect on and assess your progress. Determine if any changes are needed. Take some time here to evaluate the different areas listed below.

PROGRESS

Are you keeping up with the challenges you set, or are you failing? If you're failing, what's needed to get back on track? If you're on track, keep it going.

REFLECTIONS _____

_____

_____

_____

DIFFICULTY LEVEL

Challenges typically start out difficult and become gradually easier as you progress. Reflect on the difficulty level of your challenges. Are they too easy? Too difficult? Now is the time to increase the intensity, or scale back a bit if you bit off more than you can chew. Remember, the purpose is to challenge yourself appropriately by balancing difficulty with sustainability.

REFLECTIONS _____

_____

_____

_____

MINDSET/OTHER

How has your mindset been up to this point? Write about your mental wins or losses, what you've learned about yourself, any realizations you've had, or anything else noteworthy about your experiences so far.

REFLECTIONS _____

_____

_____

_____

___/___/ 20___

DAY TRACKER

DAY 11 OF 30

MARK AN "X" ON EACH COMPLETED CHALLENGE

CHALLENGE: #1 ☐   #2 ☐   #3 ☐   #4 ☐

DIFFICULTY LEVEL (1-10)

CHALLENGE: #1 _____   #2 _____   #3 _____   #4 _____

TIME TO COMPLETE (IF APPLICABLE)

CHALLENGE: #1 _____   #2 _____   #3 _____   #4 _____

REFLECT ON TODAY'S CHALLENGES

REFLECTIONS _____

_____

_____

_____

_____

_____

_____

_____

_____

_____

_____

_____

_____

TODAY'S OTHER CRITICAL DAILY TASKS (CDT'S)

☐ _____
☐ _____
☐ _____
☐ _____

__/__/ 20__ **DAY TRACKER** DAY 12 OF 30

MARK AN "X" ON EACH COMPLETED CHALLENGE

CHALLENGE: #1 ☐ #2 ☐ #3 ☐ #4 ☐

DIFFICULTY LEVEL (1-10)

CHALLENGE: #1 _____ #2 _____ #3 _____ #4 _____

TIME TO COMPLETE (IF APPLICABLE)

CHALLENGE: #1 _____ #2 _____ #3 _____ #4 _____

REFLECT ON TODAY'S CHALLENGES

REFLECTIONS _____

_____
_____
_____
_____
_____
_____
_____
_____
_____
_____
_____
_____
_____

TODAY'S OTHER CRITICAL DAILY TASKS (CDT'S)

☐ _____
☐ _____
☐ _____
☐ _____

___/___/ 20___ **DAY TRACKER** DAY 13 OF 30

MARK AN "X" ON EACH COMPLETED CHALLENGE

CHALLENGE: #1 ☐ #2 ☐ #3 ☐ #4 ☐

DIFFICULTY LEVEL (1-10)

CHALLENGE: #1 _____ #2 _____ #3 _____ #4 _____

TIME TO COMPLETE (IF APPLICABLE)

CHALLENGE: #1 _____ #2 _____ #3 _____ #4 _____

REFLECT ON TODAY'S CHALLENGES

REFLECTIONS _____
_____
_____
_____
_____
_____
_____
_____
_____
_____
_____
_____
_____

TODAY'S OTHER CRITICAL DAILY TASKS (CDT'S)

☐ _____
☐ _____
☐ _____
☐ _____

___/___/ 20___

DAY TRACKER

DAY 14 OF 30

MARK AN "X" ON EACH COMPLETED CHALLENGE

CHALLENGE: #1 ☐   #2 ☐   #3 ☐   #4 ☐

DIFFICULTY LEVEL (1-10)

CHALLENGE: #1 _____   #2 _____   #3 _____   #4 _____

TIME TO COMPLETE (IF APPLICABLE)

CHALLENGE: #1 _____   #2 _____   #3 _____   #4 _____

REFLECT ON TODAY'S CHALLENGES

REFLECTIONS _____

_____
_____
_____
_____
_____
_____
_____
_____
_____
_____
_____
_____

TODAY'S OTHER CRITICAL DAILY TASKS (CDT'S)

☐ _____
☐ _____
☐ _____
☐ _____

___/___/ 20___ **DAY TRACKER** DAY 15 OF 30

MARK AN "X" ON EACH COMPLETED CHALLENGE

CHALLENGE: #1 ☐ #2 ☐ #3 ☐ #4 ☐

DIFFICULTY LEVEL (1-10)

CHALLENGE: #1 _____ #2 _____ #3 _____ #4 _____

TIME TO COMPLETE (IF APPLICABLE)

CHALLENGE: #1 _____ #2 _____ #3 _____ #4 _____

REFLECT ON TODAY'S CHALLENGES

REFLECTIONS _____
_____
_____
_____
_____
_____
_____
_____
_____
_____
_____
_____
_____
_____

TODAY'S OTHER CRITICAL DAILY TASKS (CDT'S)

☐ _____
☐ _____
☐ _____
☐ _____

___/___/ 20___ **DAY TRACKER** DAY 16 OF 30

MARK AN "X" ON EACH COMPLETED CHALLENGE

CHALLENGE: #1 ☐   #2 ☐   #3 ☐   #4 ☐

DIFFICULTY LEVEL (1-10)

CHALLENGE: #1 _____   #2 _____   #3 _____   #4 _____

TIME TO COMPLETE (IF APPLICABLE)

CHALLENGE: #1 _____   #2 _____   #3 _____   #4 _____

REFLECT ON TODAY'S CHALLENGES

REFLECTIONS _____

_____
_____
_____
_____
_____
_____
_____
_____
_____
_____
_____
_____
_____

TODAY'S OTHER CRITICAL DAILY TASKS (CDT'S)

☐ _____
☐ _____
☐ _____
☐ _____

___/___/ 20___ **DAY TRACKER** DAY 17 OF 30

MARK AN "X" ON EACH COMPLETED CHALLENGE

CHALLENGE: #1 ☐ #2 ☐ #3 ☐ #4 ☐

DIFFICULTY LEVEL (1-10)

CHALLENGE: #1 _____ #2 _____ #3 _____ #4 _____

TIME TO COMPLETE (IF APPLICABLE)

CHALLENGE: #1 _____ #2 _____ #3 _____ #4 _____

REFLECT ON TODAY'S CHALLENGES

REFLECTIONS _____
_____
_____
_____
_____
_____
_____
_____
_____
_____
_____
_____
_____
_____

TODAY'S OTHER CRITICAL DAILY TASKS (CDT'S)

☐ _____
☐ _____
☐ _____
☐ _____

___/___/ 20___

DAY TRACKER

DAY 18 OF 30

MARK AN "X" ON EACH COMPLETED CHALLENGE

CHALLENGE: #1 ☐   #2 ☐   #3 ☐   #4 ☐

DIFFICULTY LEVEL (1-10)

CHALLENGE: #1 _____   #2 _____   #3 _____   #4 _____

TIME TO COMPLETE (IF APPLICABLE)

CHALLENGE: #1 _____   #2 _____   #3 _____   #4 _____

REFLECT ON TODAY'S CHALLENGES

REFLECTIONS _____

_____
_____
_____
_____
_____
_____
_____
_____
_____
_____
_____
_____

TODAY'S OTHER CRITICAL DAILY TASKS (CDT'S)

☐ _____
☐ _____
☐ _____
☐ _____

___/___/ 20___ **DAY TRACKER** DAY 19 OF 30

MARK AN "X" ON EACH COMPLETED CHALLENGE

CHALLENGE: #1 ☐   #2 ☐   #3 ☐   #4 ☐

DIFFICULTY LEVEL (1-10)

CHALLENGE: #1 _____   #2 _____   #3 _____   #4 _____

TIME TO COMPLETE (IF APPLICABLE)

CHALLENGE: #1 _____   #2 _____   #3 _____   #4 _____

REFLECT ON TODAY'S CHALLENGES

REFLECTIONS _____
_____
_____
_____
_____
_____
_____
_____
_____
_____
_____
_____
_____
_____

TODAY'S OTHER CRITICAL DAILY TASKS (CDT'S)

☐ _____
☐ _____
☐ _____
☐ _____

___/___/ 20___   **DAY TRACKER**   DAY 20 OF 30

MARK AN "X" ON EACH COMPLETED CHALLENGE

CHALLENGE: #1 ☐   #2 ☐   #3 ☐   #4 ☐

DIFFICULTY LEVEL (1-10)

CHALLENGE: #1 _____   #2 _____   #3 _____   #4 _____

TIME TO COMPLETE (IF APPLICABLE)

CHALLENGE: #1 _____   #2 _____   #3 _____   #4 _____

REFLECT ON TODAY'S CHALLENGES

REFLECTIONS _____

_____
_____
_____
_____
_____
_____
_____
_____
_____
_____
_____
_____

TODAY'S OTHER CRITICAL DAILY TASKS (CDT'S)

☐ _____
☐ _____
☐ _____
☐ _____

20 DAY ASSESSMENT

DAY 20 OF 30

You're 2/3 of the way to completing this 30 DAY CHALLENGE. Now is a great time to do another assessment of your progress and determine if any changes are needed. Take some time here to evaluate the different areas listed below.

PROGRESS

Are you keeping up with the challenges you set, or are you failing? If you're failing, what's needed to get back on track? If you're on track, keep it going.

REFLECTIONS _____

_____

_____

_____

DIFFICULTY LEVEL

You've now completed more days than you have left of this challenge. Has this been more or less difficult than you anticipated? What has been easiest and what has been hardest for you up to this point?

REFLECTIONS _____

_____

_____

_____

MINDSET/OTHER

How has your mindset been up to this point? Write about your mental wins or losses, what you've learned about yourself, any realizations you've had, or anything else noteworthy about your experience so far.

REFLECTIONS _____

_____

_____

_____

_____

_____

___/___/ 20___ **DAY TRACKER** DAY 21 OF 30

MARK AN "X" ON EACH COMPLETED CHALLENGE

CHALLENGE: #1 ☐ #2 ☐ #3 ☐ #4 ☐

DIFFICULTY LEVEL (1-10)

CHALLENGE: #1 _____ #2 _____ #3 _____ #4 _____

TIME TO COMPLETE (IF APPLICABLE)

CHALLENGE: #1 _____ #2 _____ #3 _____ #4 _____

REFLECT ON TODAY'S CHALLENGES

REFLECTIONS _____
_____
_____
_____
_____
_____
_____
_____
_____
_____
_____
_____
_____

TODAY'S OTHER CRITICAL DAILY TASKS (CDT'S)

☐ _____
☐ _____
☐ _____
☐ _____

___/___/ 20___ # DAY TRACKER DAY 22 OF 30

MARK AN "X" ON EACH COMPLETED CHALLENGE

CHALLENGE: #1 ☐   #2 ☐   #3 ☐   #4 ☐

DIFFICULTY LEVEL (1-10)

CHALLENGE: #1 _____   #2 _____   #3 _____   #4 _____

TIME TO COMPLETE (IF APPLICABLE)

CHALLENGE: #1 _____   #2 _____   #3 _____   #4 _____

REFLECT ON TODAY'S CHALLENGES

REFLECTIONS _____
_____
_____
_____
_____
_____
_____
_____
_____
_____
_____
_____
_____
_____

TODAY'S OTHER CRITICAL DAILY TASKS (CDT'S)

☐ _____
☐ _____
☐ _____
☐ _____

___/___/ 20___

DAY TRACKER

DAY 23 OF 30

MARK AN "X" ON EACH COMPLETED CHALLENGE

CHALLENGE: #1 ☐   #2 ☐   #3 ☐   #4 ☐

DIFFICULTY LEVEL (1-10)

CHALLENGE: #1 _____   #2 _____   #3 _____   #4 _____

TIME TO COMPLETE (IF APPLICABLE)

CHALLENGE: #1 _____   #2 _____   #3 _____   #4 _____

REFLECT ON TODAY'S CHALLENGES

REFLECTIONS _____

_____
_____
_____
_____
_____
_____
_____
_____
_____
_____
_____
_____
_____

TODAY'S OTHER CRITICAL DAILY TASKS (CDT'S)

☐ _____
☐ _____
☐ _____
☐ _____

___/___/ 20___ **DAY TRACKER** DAY 24 OF 30

MARK AN "X" ON EACH COMPLETED CHALLENGE

CHALLENGE: #1 ☐   #2 ☐   #3 ☐   #4 ☐

DIFFICULTY LEVEL (1-10)

CHALLENGE: #1 _____   #2 _____   #3 _____   #4 _____

TIME TO COMPLETE (IF APPLICABLE)

CHALLENGE: #1 _____   #2 _____   #3 _____   #4 _____

REFLECT ON TODAY'S CHALLENGES

REFLECTIONS _____
_____
_____
_____
_____
_____
_____
_____
_____
_____
_____
_____
_____
_____

TODAY'S OTHER CRITICAL DAILY TASKS (CDT'S)

☐ _____
☐ _____
☐ _____
☐ _____

__/__/ 20__ **DAY TRACKER** DAY 25 OF 30

MARK AN "X" ON EACH COMPLETED CHALLENGE

CHALLENGE: #1 ☐ #2 ☐ #3 ☐ #4 ☐

DIFFICULTY LEVEL (1-10)

CHALLENGE: #1 _____ #2 _____ #3 _____ #4 _____

TIME TO COMPLETE (IF APPLICABLE)

CHALLENGE: #1 _____ #2 _____ #3 _____ #4 _____

REFLECT ON TODAY'S CHALLENGES

REFLECTIONS _____

_____
_____
_____
_____
_____
_____
_____
_____
_____
_____
_____
_____
_____

TODAY'S OTHER CRITICAL DAILY TASKS (CDT'S)

☐ _____
☐ _____
☐ _____
☐ _____

___/___/20___   # DAY TRACKER   DAY 26 OF 30

MARK AN "X" ON EACH COMPLETED CHALLENGE

CHALLENGE: #1 ☐   #2 ☐   #3 ☐   #4 ☐

DIFFICULTY LEVEL (1-10)

CHALLENGE: #1 _____   #2 _____   #3 _____   #4 _____

TIME TO COMPLETE (IF APPLICABLE)

CHALLENGE: #1 _____   #2 _____   #3 _____   #4 _____

REFLECT ON TODAY'S CHALLENGES

REFLECTIONS _____

_____

_____

_____

_____

_____

_____

_____

_____

_____

_____

_____

TODAY'S OTHER CRITICAL DAILY TASKS (CDT'S)

☐ _____
☐ _____
☐ _____
☐ _____

___/___/ 20___

DAY TRACKER

DAY 27 OF 30

MARK AN "X" ON EACH COMPLETED CHALLENGE

CHALLENGE: #1 ☐   #2 ☐   #3 ☐   #4 ☐

DIFFICULTY LEVEL (1-10)

CHALLENGE: #1 _____   #2 _____   #3 _____   #4 _____

TIME TO COMPLETE (IF APPLICABLE)

CHALLENGE: #1 _____   #2 _____   #3 _____   #4 _____

REFLECT ON TODAY'S CHALLENGES

REFLECTIONS _____
_____
_____
_____
_____
_____
_____
_____
_____
_____
_____
_____
_____
_____

TODAY'S OTHER CRITICAL DAILY TASKS (CDT'S)

☐ _____
☐ _____
☐ _____
☐ _____

___/___/ 20___   **DAY TRACKER**   DAY 28 OF 30

MARK AN "X" ON EACH COMPLETED CHALLENGE

CHALLENGE: #1 ☐   #2 ☐   #3 ☐   #4 ☐

DIFFICULTY LEVEL (1-10)

CHALLENGE: #1 _____   #2 _____   #3 _____   #4 _____

TIME TO COMPLETE (IF APPLICABLE)

CHALLENGE: #1 _____   #2 _____   #3 _____   #4 _____

REFLECT ON TODAY'S CHALLENGES

REFLECTIONS _____
_____
_____
_____
_____
_____
_____
_____
_____
_____
_____
_____
_____
_____

TODAY'S OTHER CRITICAL DAILY TASKS (CDT'S)

☐ _____
☐ _____
☐ _____
☐ _____

___/___/ 20___

DAY TRACKER

DAY 29 OF 30

MARK AN "X" ON EACH COMPLETED CHALLENGE

CHALLENGE: #1 ☐ #2 ☐ #3 ☐ #4 ☐

DIFFICULTY LEVEL (1-10)

CHALLENGE: #1 _____ #2 _____ #3 _____ #4 _____

TIME TO COMPLETE (IF APPLICABLE)

CHALLENGE: #1 _____ #2 _____ #3 _____ #4 _____

REFLECT ON TODAY'S CHALLENGES

REFLECTIONS _____
_____
_____
_____
_____
_____
_____
_____
_____
_____
_____
_____
_____

TODAY'S OTHER CRITICAL DAILY TASKS (CDT'S)

☐ _____
☐ _____
☐ _____
☐ _____

___/___/20___ **DAY TRACKER** DAY 30 OF 30

MARK AN "X" ON EACH COMPLETED CHALLENGE

CHALLENGE: #1 ☐   #2 ☐   #3 ☐   #4 ☐

DIFFICULTY LEVEL (1-10)

CHALLENGE: #1 _____   #2 _____   #3 _____   #4 _____

TIME TO COMPLETE (IF APPLICABLE)

CHALLENGE: #1 _____   #2 _____   #3 _____   #4 _____

REFLECT ON TODAY'S CHALLENGES

REFLECTIONS _____
_____
_____
_____
_____
_____
_____
_____
_____
_____
_____
_____
_____
_____

TODAY'S OTHER CRITICAL DAILY TASKS (CDT'S)

☐ _____
☐ _____
☐ _____
☐ _____

30 DAY ASSESSMENT

DAY 30 OF 30

Congratulations! You've completed this 30 DAY CHALLENGE. Take some time here to evaluate the different areas listed below.

AREAS OF GROWTH

After completing each challenge over the last 30 days, where have you noticed the most growth in your life? How is your life different now compared to 30 days ago?

REFLECTIONS _____
_____
_____
_____
_____
_____

ROOM FOR IMPROVEMENT

We can always identify areas in which we could have done better. If you were to do this same challenge over again, what would you do differently?

REFLECTIONS _____
_____
_____
_____
_____

WHAT'S NEXT?

These 30 DAY CHALLENGES are not meant to be completed and then have you go back to your old ways. Keep your momentum going by planning out and writing down some ideas for your next 30 DAY CHALLENGE below. Use the "Notes" pages at the end if you need more room.

REFLECTIONS _____
_____
_____
_____

> "WE ARE WHAT WE REPEATEDLY DO. THEREFORE, EXCELLENCE IS NOT AN ACT, BUT A HABIT."
>
> — ARISTOTLE

OMEGA & ALPHA

First off, congratulations on making it through this 30 DAY CHALLENGE! If you're reading this, it's probably safe to say you completed it with success. It's likely that most people who buy this journal never complete it. So again, congrats on making it this far.

If you set appropriate challenges, disciplined yourself to complete them regularly, and finished strong, it's all but guaranteed you have made progress from where you were. You are 30 days closer to the person you want to be!

"Omega" is the Greek word for "the end". "Alpha" is the Greek word for "the beginning". That's exactly what this is. There is truly no such thing as elimination in life; there is only replacement. The end of one thing is always the beginning of another.

Reaching the end of this 30 DAY CHALLENGE is the end of something, but it should also be the beginning of the next. To allow the completion of this 30 DAY CHALLENGE to be your "Omega" would be a total shame and arguably a total waste of time and energy. Your elephant is not yet eaten.

None of what you just completed in the last 30 days matters if this is where you leave it. If you decide to throw in the towel, go back to your old habits and ways of living, this sense of accomplishment and progress that you feel right now will become merely a memory in a short amount of time. The pride and satisfaction will soon sour and turn to regret and self-loathing because you showed yourself what you were capable of, but then failed to maintain it. You will become upset if this 30 DAY CHALLENGE is all the journey ever was. 30 days is just the beginning. Remember, the pain of discipline weighs ounces, but the pain of regret weighs tons.

OMEGA & ALPHA

So keep this momentum going! The race has just begun. The road has just been discovered and embarked upon. You don't want to just be average or forgettable. You want to be powerful, impactful, memorable, and comprehensive.

ASK YOURSELF:
-If I were to die today, would I be proud of my life or ashamed of it?
-Did I use my talents, gifts, and abilities to their fullest potential, or did I squander them by living small and playing it safe?
-What do I want people to say about me at my funeral?
-What would they actually say if they had all taken a truth serum?
-What would they write on my headstone or in my obituary?

This is your legacy. You only get one shot at it. Make it one of pride, honor, accomplishment, discipline, and heroism. You are the hero in your story. Let this be just the beginning. Let this be a step along the path less traveled. Keep moving forward and keep eating your elephant, one bite at a time.

Reflect. Strategize. Execute. Repeat. If you failed more often than you succeeded at your challenges, or if you fell off altogether, admit it, accept it, assess it, adjust it, and get back to it. The only true, lasting failure is giving up. If you end on a failure and decide to stay a quitter, you're bound for a life of mediocrity at best. Every successful person, regardless of their successes, has a long list of failures, disappointments, and setbacks behind them. They are inevitable, but they are also temporary. The important takeaway is to learn from them and keep moving forward. In the same way good habits multiply, the same is true for bad habits.

Remember your "Why's". Remember the purpose of any challenge is to change your identity and become the person you wish to be.

The elephant must get eaten. Don't put down that fork.

NOTES

NOTES

NOTES

NOTES